MW00883918

Dancing
with
LANDMINES

YVONNE CAMPBELL

Dancing with Landmines
By Yvonne Campbell
Copyright 2019, Yvonne Campbell
All Rights Reserved

Disclaimer:
This is a work of fiction. Names, characters, businesses, places, events, locales, and incidents are either the products of the author's imagination or used in a fictitious manner. Any resemblance to actual persons, living or dead, or actual events is purely coincidental.

No part of this publication may be reproduced, stored in a retrieval system or transmitted in any way by any means, electronic, mechanical, photocopy, recording or otherwise without the prior permission of the author except as provided by USA copyright law.

Interior Design: Ellen Sallas, The Author's Mentor, www.theauthorsmentor.com
Cover Photo © Michael Simons, 123rf.com
Cover Graphic Design: Elizabeth E. Little, Hyliian.deviantart.com

ISBN-13: 9781095565155

Also available in eBook

PUBLISHED IN THE UNITED STATES OF AMERICA

DEDICATION

This book is dedicated My Lord and Savior, Jesus Christ. Thank You for being ever-present in my life. Thank You for calling me worthy to suffer persecution and giving me this wonderful testimony. Thank You for using me to help others.

Lord, I thank You for my family: my loving and compassionate husband, Jack, my wonderful gifts You gave me in my children, Kavan, Kyndale, and Ashley, and of course, blessing me with my first grandson, Grayson.

Dancing
with
LANDMINES

Table of Contents

Introduction

...from the Author

Throughout my life I have had one testimony after another. Then it hit me that God must have a great purpose for my life, because He has sustained me even when I wasn't living to honor Him. I started writing this book after my divorce that was final in 1999. I changed the actual names to keep the privacy of others, but this is my autobiography. My friends and family would always tell me that my life could've been a good book or an off the hook movie, because all the things that have happened to me and I am still sane, couldn't do anything but help someone else through their struggles, and let somebody know that "YOU ARE NOT ALONE". I never thought I would have made it through it all. I thank My HEAVENLY FATHER for carrying the weight on my shoulders, because I know that it wasn't me on my own. I am but a frail woman. There were many days that I wanted to give up, but MY FATHER kept assisting me, and lifting me. I thank Him for where I am today, and for the testimony I am about to give to you. In my life I've learned that everything happens for a reason, and with each occurrence we need to be able to take some education for every aspect of our lives, and retain them and save that knowledge, because it will assist us with a bigger task in the future. Just make sure you put GOD first in your life and you'll be able to see all the many blessing HE will give you. MY HEAVENLY FATHER is so worthy to be praised! Why don't you go ahead and praise him for everything he's done in your life!

1

From the Beginning

Well as far as I can remember. I always wanted to be just like my mother. As a child I used to dress in her clothes and mock her mannerisms. My mother and I used to be like sisters. We used to confide in each other, but like many single mothers she had to do whatever it took to make ends meet.

I really don't remember much about my childhood before I was about four or five. I recall I attended a preschool called Little Angels in Highland Park, Michigan. At that time, we lived in an apartment building on Moss in Highland Park, Michigan, also. I remember there were orange and green circle patterns on the walls. Our apartment had a living room, a small kitchen with a nice size window by the table and of course a bathroom, but it's unclear to me if there were one or two bedrooms.

My mother and I lived there. I remember having my only Christmas that I recall with my mother there. I remember getting a train set. I am not sure how long we stayed there, but the only other home I remembered us having together was on Fenmore in Detroit, Michigan.

On Detroit's west side, Seven Mile, and Southfield freeway area, we moved into a corner house that was white and green. It had a living room that you entered coming through the front door. The kitchen was on the back side of the house with a hallway connecting the only bathroom and two bedrooms. The basement was open, and the backyard was huge with a very tall pine tree in the center of the backyard and a cherry tree to the side near the back gate. I have only a few memories here but much more than before. I remember my mother got me a swing set for the backyard and every time my cousins and I would swing it would pop up.

I remember my cousins and I climbing the cherry tree and eating cherries until we could eat no more. I remember my mother, my cousins and I having a leaf fight. I remember walking up to the library by myself.

I had a best friend named Brad Hunter. He had a brother Mark and his mother was Dawn and his dad was Brad, Sr. I remember always enjoying spending time at their house. We would play all kinds of games and swing on their swing set. Dawn and Brad Sr. were the greatest parents; Dawn used to cut the edges off the sandwiches and she had the prettiest dimples. I remember Brad, Sr. was very funny and kept us laughing. I also recall that their house was brown and yellow.

I had to be about six or seven when I attended Fox

Elementary. I really get a blur, but I do recall that I had two Caucasian teachers that I liked a lot. I remember that the school had portables. I do remember playing the violin, but as far as which school, I am not sure. I remember later attending Bow Elementary. I remember that my life was great, really easygoing, and stress-free.

2

The Introduction of Change

One day, my mother took me skating at Wheels Roller Rink on Schoolcraft in Detroit, Michigan. This is where my life began to change. This guy approached me; he had to be about eighteen or nineteen years old. At this time, I was maybe eight or nine, but I happened to be very busty and filled out. He asked me to skate. I told him he would have to ask my mother. When he did, she intervened and allowed him to skate with her instead. To add a little insight on everything, my mother had me when she was sixteen so all she ever told me was stay away from guys. At this time, my mother was about twenty-four and I had no idea that this guy would become my stepfather.

Lorenzo Leroy Brown was his name. I guess they used to spend a lot of time together, but I had no knowledge of it because I spent a lot of time at my grandmother's house.

I recall the day that we were formally introduced. My mother and I went to pick him up from his mother's house where he lived. I used to always ride shotgun, but out of respect for adults I got in the back and sat up between the two seats. When he got into the car they kissed, and I made sound like I was getting sick. He turned to me and said with several curse words, "Shut up and sit back!"

I was speechless. I looked at my mother and she didn't respond. This was nothing like my mother, so I asked her whether she heard what he said. She didn't respond so I turned and told him as rude and abrasive as he was to me that I didn't know who he thought he was, but I wasn't going to let him talk to me that way. I then turned to my mother and requested to be dropped off to my grandmother.

I am not sure if there was any conversation that followed, but I do remember spending a lot more time at my grandmother's house after that.

I loved my grandmother. We used to go shopping together, we sat and drank tea out of her best China, sometimes, we'd decorate the table with beautiful dishes and just sit and talk. I also spent a lot of time with my cousins, Derek, Deana, and Connie. We were around each other so much it was like they were my siblings. They didn't stay there with Grandma, but just like me they were always there visiting.

3

Aunt Rita's House

My cousins' mother, Aunt Rita, used to live on Woodland in Highland Park, Michigan, in a big house with three floors and several entrances. We used to scare each other saying ghosts were haunting that house.

Aunt Rita was a chain-smoker. One day I got curious and lit up one of the butts in the ash tray. Before I could even puff good, Aunt Rita came out of nowhere, whooped my butt and threatened me, "If I ever catch you smoking again, I will kick you're a**!!!" I guess it worked because I never had or wanted to smoke again. I even dislike smoke in my presence.

The very next place I remember them staying was on Miller in Detroit, Michigan. It was a two-family flat. It had a living room, dining room, a big kitchen and two bedrooms, and of course a huge bathroom. Aunt Rita used to be asleep all the time and for the most part, we behaved and played amongst ourselves. One day Derek, Deana and I were listening to the radio and "777-9311," a new song, came on the radio. We decided to call the operator and sing to her. Deana and I sang "7-7-7-93-11, and Derek sang "I wanna spend the night with you if that's alright!" We laughed and hung up the phone and went back to playing something else. The operator called back to inform my aunt that we were playing on the phone. When she came to us to see who it was, no one fessed up. She lined all of us up, even Connie, who had been somewhere reading. We started to tell the truth, but she still went down the line. Everybody was getting it. When she got to me, I was so scared that I was screaming and kicking, and I ended up kicking her hard in the nose. She started screaming that she was going to kill me. We all ran around the corner to one of my cousin's friend's house and called Grandma to get us.

Aunt Rita later moved to Ryan Street, and had a three-bedroom gray and black frame bungalow. I guess by the time she moved there we were beginning to grow up. Aunt Rita was still always sleeping, and the house was always cold, but we managed to stay out of trouble.

4

Her Wedding

It had to be no more than a couple months that they had been dating when my mother came to me to tell me that she and Leroy were getting married.

She said I was going to be in the wedding and hold her train. I told her, "You couldn't be getting married already; you barely even know him."

She replied we are getting married and you will hold my train, and her girlfriend was already making me the cutest sundress.

I told her that I wasn't going to be in her wedding, and I didn't care if her train was drug in the mud, I wasn't carrying it. I told her I didn't even want to come to the wedding.

She responded, "You don't have a choice. What are you going to do? I'm getting married in your grandmother's front room."

Just as she said, they held the wedding at Grandmother's house. I was there in the dress that her friend made, but not carrying her train. I sat in the big chair in the front room and slept through the whole thing. My grandmother woke me after it was over. I changed my clothes and the rest of that day was just a blur.

5

The Southern Move

Not long after my mother Martha Debbie Williams-Brown and her husband got married my mother's father became very sick with cancer. He was living in Memphis, Tennessee at the time. My mother felt that she needed to be close to her father, so she relocated us to Tennessee. I tried talking to her. I told her I didn't want to live with her and him. I told her that all my friends and family were here. I told her I didn't even know her father so being close to him was only important to her. It didn't matter; she had made up her mind that I was not going to stay in Detroit with my grandmother. I was going to Memphis with her and her husband. She sold the house that she always said was mine and I had no input or choice in the matter.

We ended up moving into the Hillview Apartments. I didn't have many friends, but I ended up having a crush on the guy next door. We used to sit on the porch and laugh and sing, but when my mother decided to pay some attention, I was forbidden to talk to him anymore.

Shortly after that, we moved into a duplex around the corner from Aunt Mary, Anna, Piper, and Jill. It was a wooded subdivision with winding streets. The closest store was on the other end of the woods. Shortly after we moved there, my mother's father died.

6

The Non-Family Member

After the death of my mother's father life began to change. My mother had Annette Debbie Brown, my younger sister, with a 10-year difference. My mother began to get her priorities into place and it seemed that I was on the bottom of the list. Her husband came first, Annette came second, and if there was any time left, she'd talk at me. She gave off the impression that I was invading her newfound family, as if I was some sort of outsider and in the way. I began to develop my own life. I had friends she didn't know and when I went away, she didn't even notice my absence. I started asking questions about my father.

7

Hunting for A Lost Cause

I ended up wondering if my father knew anything about me, and if he did… Why hadn't he been around? I started probing for information from my mother. She always said she knew who he was and that he was always a good father to his kids. But what about me? I decided to write him a letter. His name was Nicholas Green, and he lived in Detroit, Michigan. He was supposedly an executive for General Motors. He was also described as a rolling stone; I was told I had four sisters all by different women.

Well, instead of him responding to my letter, he came to visit me in Memphis. This was the first time I recalled seeing him. I had to be about twelve years old. We sat in his car and talked. He told me that he wasn't my father. He said that my mother and him had gone to Friends of The Court and at that time no blood test was done, but the court decided he was not my father. I was puzzled. He ended up getting my hair done and gave me some money and that was it.

Shortly after that visit my mother found out she was pregnant with my second sister, Linda Rachel Brown. I gave up on any time we might spend together and started looking for attention and love in other places.

8

As Long as You Didn't Start It

We finally moved into a house on Rutgers Street. It was a ranch style house with three bedrooms and a huge backyard that had its own orchard. There were apple trees, plum trees, nectarine trees and a strawberry patch. I had just begun the seventh grade and I was still like the new girl from Detroit. All the guys wanted to be with me and all the girls wanted to beat me up.

Coincidentally this was the year I had my first fight in school. It happened to have nothing to do with my home life. This girl was jealous of me and had no other reason to want to beat me up, but she taunted me all day long saying, "After school I am gonna kick your butt!"

I never said anything to her or anyone else about the threats, I just continued with my day. My last class was art and the hall was more crowded than usual. I looked to the end of the hall and there she was waiting for me. I was scared and I still didn't know what I did to her. As I walked up the hallway other students started grabbing my book bag, my books and my jacket, but when they reached for my purse, I wouldn't let it go. It wasn't for some sort of protection; it was because everything that was important to me was in there and I didn't want to lose it.

The girl ran toward me and I reacted. I started swinging and punching, and before I knew it, I had kicked her butt. She was on the floor under me and then a teacher took us to the office. I sat there emotionless until they said they were going to call my mother. I was so scared of what she would do to me. When she arrived and talked to the principal, she asked me only one question: "Did you win?" When I told her "Yes!" she replied, "As long as you didn't start it, but you finished it, you don't have anything to worry about."

We ended up going out shopping for the rest of the day. I couldn't remember spending this kind of time with my mother alone. We actually had fun. From that day on, she started coming up to my school frequently.

9

Finding Lil' Red

By this time, I was into makeup, money, and boys. My mother put me on complete lockdown. No phone calls, no visits and nothing pertaining to a guy. One day my mother and I were in the mall and a guy from my school spoke to me. All he said was, "Hi, Yvonne!" My mother smacked me hard and then asked me why he was talking to me. From that point I tried to stay out of their sight so that I could stay out of trouble.

You see, my mother had me at sixteen and my father was thirty. She was worried that I'd go down the same path as she did. I used to always tell her that if I put my mind to doing something, nothing that she did could stop me from accomplishing my goal. She stayed on my back constantly. I ended up messing around with the class clown; his name was Mike. He wasn't attractive, but I knew that he lived around the corner from me and he was already having sex. I figured that one day I would get the nerves and give him my virginity so the next time my mother said something about me losing my virginity, I'd tell her I already gave it away. I thought maybe then she'd get off my back. So, one day his mother went out of town, and we did it.

Afterwards, Mike started dogging me out and showing out on me in front of his friends. All my friends were guys and when the word spread around school, they began devise a plan to deal with him.

At the end of the school day as I got on the bus, Mike was already on it and showing out. As I found a seat he approached and smacked me. Before I had a chance to respond, guys came from all over the school parking lot and from other buses, grabbed Mike and drug him into the woods. I am not sure what happened out there, but when Mike returned to school, his leg was in a cast.

10

Growing Up Fast

After all the smoke cleared about Mike, my mother found out what happened. Mike used to hang out across the street from my house. She was on the phone talking to someone and I heard her storm out the front door and head across the street. I ran out of my room after her, but she was already confronting him about putting his hands on me. She had him up against the house and she basically threatened his life. She made him apologize, but she had only gotten half of the story. I had been waiting so long to tell her about losing my virginity, but I didn't want him to die that day by my mother.

We made it back in the house and she wanted to hear my side of the story. I told her. She looked so disappointed; she put me on punishment and sent me to my room. I didn't mind that; I pretty much was always in my room making Barbie doll clothes, writing poetry or listening to my radio. To compensate for that, she decided that all my Barbie dolls could be played with by my little sisters and then she broke all my records. My room was no longer my personal area; if Annette and Linda wanted to come in my room, I couldn't stop them. My mother said it was because every room in the house belonged to her anyway.

So I dealt with the cards I was given. I started dating and having boyfriends that my family had no clue of. One day we were all going skating and I had set up to meet my boyfriend Tony Young. My mother started ranting and raving that I needed to put a sweater on. It had to be about 75 or 80 degrees. I debated that I didn't need a sweater. She told me put on a jacket or sweater or stay home. I went in my room really frustrated but trying to obey. I couldn't find anything quickly and she was rushing me. I grabbed a pullover and ran to the door. My mother was standing there, and she said, "Oh! So now you want to be smart!" She snatched my purse and punched me in the face hollering, "Give me my keys and get out of my house!"

I was hurt and crying, mainly because I knew that I wouldn't see Tony for some time now. She kicked me out and I started running.

11

Wolf in Sheep's Clothing

It had to be about 8pm as I ran to the corner. I heard my stepfather Leroy calling after me, telling me to come back. I didn't want to be there. I definitely didn't feel like dealing with them that night. When I made it to the corner it was dark, but I knew the neighborhood. I stopped and sat next to a bush. He came running around the corner and stopped as soon as he got out of my mother's eyesight. He acted like he was hollering for me, but then without knowing I could hear him he said, "Yeah! Runaway. I don't want you in my house no way." I wasn't surprised, but it just helped reality set in. I ended up going over one of my girlfriend's house. Her mother let me stay the night, but the next day, she helped me find a shelter. I couldn't have been there for more than three days when my mother found out where I was and came and got me. I ended up going back home to my punishment and lockdowns with additional chores.

12

Someone I Could Depend On

My punishment after I returned from the shelter was no radio, no privacy, free babysitting, cutting the acres of grass with a push mower, hand-washing clothes, and no bus ride to school. I had to walk two miles both ways.

I ended up walking home from school one day after a pep-rally that I finally got a chance to perform in. My girl, Maria, and I were walking home with a group of people. Two guys in a candy-apple-red convertible Mustang pulled up and the driver was flirting with me. He offered me a ride home a couple times before. I finally told him, "If you take me and my girl," and he agreed. I sat in the front and his friend got in the back.

We exchanged introductions. His name was Aaron Richards and we ended up really hitting it off. He would pick me up from school every day and we would spend some time together. We talked about my home life and he always told me to keep my head up. He always told me he would be there for me. He gave me a cell phone to call him whenever I needed to.

13

The Rumble in the Bedroom

My stepfather had become a lot blunter about how he felt about me. He used to buy food and get an attitude if I ate something. One day I came from the Kingdom Hall and grabbed a small bag of chips to eat. He ranted and raved about the 25-cent bag of chips. I told him I would replace it. It was just something quick to eat. He said, "I brought those chips for my kids to have whenever they wanted them, not for you to just pick up and eat." I told him if I knew it was going to cause all this trouble, I wouldn't have even touched them. He sent me to my room and told me to take my clothes off; he was going to whoop me. I told him, "I don't think so!"

I went to my room and went to change out of my dress clothes. He burst in my room unannounced. I was standing there in my bra and panties. I had to be at least fourteen years old and him twenty-four. I pushed him back out and locked my door. I told him, "I am too old for you to be busting in unannounced!"

He kicked the door in with my mother standing there screaming, "Take your punishment!" I told him he wasn't supposed to be in my room while I wasn't dressed. He swung the belt at me and we began to tussle. Each time he hit me I hit him back. I ended up breaking his glasses, tearing up his suit, and getting on with the punishment. My mother had revealed that I wasn't as important to her as she claimed.

Before this incident, we ended up spending the night over Leroy's parents' house. I don't remember why, but I remember all the adults were downstairs playing cards. I was either sent to bed or just wanted to get away from everybody. I was sleep on his sister's floor on a pallet. I remember trying to turn over, but someone was on both sides of me. My panties were down, and his brother and brother-in-law were on either side of me. I don't know if I was penetrated, but they were pulling up their pants.

His brother-in-law said, "Shh!"

I told him that if he didn't move, I was going to scream. His brother told me that no one would believe me, and they left. In the morning, I pulled my mother to the side and told her. She acted like she didn't care. Nothing happened, and from that point, I had to fend for myself. After that night, I refused to go over there, and if she made me, I would just sit in the car.

14

Involuntary Relocation

Now I was in the 9th grade and I still had to walk home and to school as a punishment. I was doing great in school and loved it. One reason was because I was able to get away from everyday life.

Aaron was twenty years old. He had his own bi-level home, three cars, and worked for the Ford dealership up the way. He listened to my problems and always tried to solve them, so when my mother would put me out, he would be the one I called to come get me. It got so regular that Aaron took me shopping to get some clothes and things to leave at his house. Once when I was at his house he taught me to drive a 5-speed and gave me the Mustang to get back and forth to school.

The last time my mother put me out in the street, I had Aaron pick me up and I stayed with him for about six weeks. It was imperative that I continued my education if I was going to be with him, so every day, I worked at the mall Dairy Queen after school. My mother never came to the school to look for me; I guess she assumed that I would just be a drop out. Once my mother found out that I had someone else to turn to, she forced me back home.

The next morning, she woke me up and told to get out of bed and head outside. Leroy's stepfather was taking me to Detroit to my grandmother. I couldn't be any more uncomfortable. I didn't trust him at all. I was sent with whatever I wore out of the house, and nothing more.

My mother got Aaron's phone numbers out of my things I left behind. She called him and told him that he better not call me, come see me, or even communicate with me or she'd make sure he'd go to jail for statutory rape. Then she lied on me and told him that I was sleeping with several guys in the neighborhood.

I made it to my grandmother's house, and she welcomed me with open arms. My grandmother and my Aunt Kelly took me shopping to get enough clothes to get me through a school week. I finally got a chance to call Aaron, and he told me what my mother told him and refused to even deal with me anymore.

15

Sophomore Year

I enrolled myself in Denby High School and never missed a beat. My cousin Derek, who everyone thought we were twins, went to the same school. All the girls were jealous of me and thought that I was trying to "take their man". All the guys were into me, because I was different and fresh meat.

I remembered one day I was headed to class and a group of girls blocked my way to class. This one girl stepped up and wanted me to explain what made me think that I was going to take her man from her. I asked her what she was talking about. She said, "Now you want to act like you ain't trying to get with Derek?" I said, "Are you crazy? Derek is my cousin! I am the last person you need to be checking. You need to see if he is really YOUR man."

She continued to try to front me off. I told her, "Don't even worry about it. Tomorrow you will be history. Leave it up to me." Later that day, I told my cousin what happened and he left her alone.

The curriculum at Denby was a lot slower than down South, so I didn't have to concentrate on school as much as everyone else. I signed up for driver's training. My teacher was Mr. Henry. My first day in class I sat back and watched. The only reason I was taking the class was because it was required to get your driver's license, although I had already been driving well. I noticed this guy named Terrance Blunt that everyone called Ricky. All the girls had bets on who was going to get with him. At the time, "New Edition," a R&B singing group, was out. He looked like Ralph Tresvant, the lead singer. I made it my goal that before the semester was over that he was going to be my boyfriend.

His brother Smitty was in the same class. One day he stopped me and asked if I would consider tutoring his brother. I asked him why he was talking to me for his brother. He told me that his brother was shy, but if he didn't pass a couple classes he would repeat 10th grade. I ended up calling him and went by his house so that we could study. That ended up being the beginning of a long and tiring relationship.

16

Shadow of a Man

A spineless, shadow of a man. My mother loved him so much because he reminded her of her husband, whatever she says, goes. Ricky and I were together five years, off and on. We used to skip school every day. I don't think I attended 10th grade any more than two months of the school year, but I passed with perfect attendance and honor roll. I used to get a pass from my geometry teacher. She used to say that you'll never use geometry in life, and gave me a pass, "To go to my boyfriend's house." Looking back at that year, I regret skipping school and even being involved with him.

I ended up getting pregnant, and when I told him I was pregnant he showed out at school. We got into an argument and he pushed me down a flight of stairs, and said, "I bet you won't be pregnant for long." I got up crying, because I thought he loved me. He and his crew turned and walked away. I left school and walked home. I stayed home for maybe two weeks and I don't think anyone even noticed. I was sitting talking to one of the older guys in the neighborhood and told him how scared and alone I felt. I told him if I could make this go away I would, but I didn't have any money. He told me to get in his truck and took me to an abortion clinic and gave me the money. He told me that he'd come and get me when I was done. He hugged me and gave me the number to reach him. Sitting in that clinic really changed my outlook on life. When everything was over, I ended up changing schools for the next school year and leaving the past behind me.

When Christmas rolled around, I got a knock at the door. It was Ricky. He had a new look. He looked like "Kwame," a hip-hop artist out at that time. He stood at the door looking over my shoulder for some signs of a baby. I lied and told him that I had a miscarriage, because of all the stress he put me through. He begged to be back with me and that he was so sorry for his actions. After some time we got back together, but broke up three times over.

The first time I remember him and his mother and younger brother Smitty living together in this little house. He would make every attempt to keep me happy, but deep down he wasn't the guy that I wanted. I always wanted a man that was kind, considerate of my feelings, and romantic, but I also wanted to be able to hold a conversation with him without having to limit my vocabulary. I needed a man with some sort of backbone. We eventually broke up and went our separate ways.

17

Junior Year

The school year began and I wanted things to be very different from when I was at Denby. I enrolled at Osborn High School, and because it wasn't in my area I had to get staff permission. I spoke with the assistant principal and all he asked for was my report card from last year. He looked at it and said, "We definitely need more people like you in this school! Welcome to Osborn!" Like I said before even though I only attended school for two months out of the year, I passed with perfect attendance and honor roll.

I wanted people to remember me after I graduated so I got involved in Concert Choir, PA Announcer, Stage Crew, Omega and became captain of the Cheerleaders. I came to Osborn for two reasons; my best friend Angel Caldwell and this new guy I was dating, Isaiah Long.

Angel lived across the street and we used to hang out a lot until her mother decided she wanted her to stop hanging out with me. Angel's mother was abusive to her mentally and physically, and Angel used to tell me everything she did to her. Her mother found out and separated us, and refused to let her communicate with me. Also, when she got wind of me attending Osborn, Angel's mother moved her out of that school.

Isaiah and I met on the Smart bus. I was working at Burger King and he was working at McDonald's. We ended up spending every waking moment together. So of course, I thought it would be cool if we were at the same school. Everything was going fine until I told him I was pregnant. I actually was over his house having dinner with his family. The first thing that came out his mouth was, "It ain't mine!" I couldn't believe he said that. Every free moment we were together. I ended up talking to his parents and his mother said, "Are you sure it is his?" His dad was just nonchalant. I left heartbroken and couldn't believe I was in this situation again.

One day I was sitting on the front porch and my grandmother came out with soup and crackers. I told her, "I never said I was hungry." She replied, "You never said you was pregnant either." I was shocked, "How did you know?" We sat down and talked, and she told me to go and speak to him again. She said if he still isn't any help, she'll pay for the abortion if I promised to be finished with him. And that is exactly how it went.

I put my head back into school and tried to excel in anything I put my hands on. By me being a cheerleader, I was semi-popular and had many friends. Anyone who was into some sort of sports, we stuck together. Isaiah and I never talked and I guess he didn't like the fact that I left him alone. One day he cornered me by my locker and tried to intimidate me. The captain of the football team found out and a few of the football players dealt with him. He was forced to apologize to me, but I was shocked to hear the captain say, "Now get over here and apologize to my girlfriend!"

I didn't say anything and accepted the apology. It was inevitable that the captain of the cheerleaders and the captain of the football team would be a couple. We ended up having a lot of fun, but still broke up after the Christmas break. He was lying and cheating on me with this girl named Yvette. Over the break she got pregnant. The way I found out was rough—I was holding his books and accidentally dropped them. A love letter from her to him fell out. I dumped him in the gym in front of everyone.

I started hanging out more with Alisha, Tina, Toni, Tika, Latonya, and Cindy. I spent all my time either at work or at school. After the games, I'd treat something to eat for those that didn't have enough money. My love was cheerleading and gymnastics, which was ironic because I had no rhythm. I couldn't dance, but I was good at cheerleading and gymnastics.

18

The Winter Bus Ride

Alisha, Tina and I met at a basketball game between Osborn and Cody High School, these guys on the west side that were putting together a rap group called P.I. By all of us being cheerleaders, they wanted us to be background dancers. I really wasn't with it, but I thought the lead rapper, James, was so fine and if this could get me and him hooked up, I was all for it. Alisha fell for Hunter and Tina was dating Eric. Tina would borrow her uncle's car and pick all of us up to take us to practice.

We ended up buying matching Gold and Black Guess outfits. I had my jacket airbrushed with a black-on-black Mustang convertible with the saying, "TOO HOT TO HANDLE, TOO COLD TO HOLD". It was the perfect saying for me as well as the car on my jacket. I only remember two different concerts that P.I. was in. We actually had a good time, and I got the attention I wanted, so it was great with me.

I remember that we used to meet at Eric's house, but one day nothing seemed to be going right. Eric and Tina broke up, so we no longer had a ride to the west side. So we ended up spending the weekend over at Eric's house. That very same day James's ex-girlfriend was there and it was very uncomfortable. She did a lot of begging and pleading for James to take her back, but that didn't work so she started showering him with gifts. I told her he couldn't accept anything from her, so she decided to buy me gifts every time she brought him a gift. She left the house and came back with groceries to cook dinner. I had never seen anyone this desperate and pathetic. Alisha and I ended up catching a cab back home. That cab ride was paid by the guys, but it was a lot of money.

The next weekend Alisha and I were supposed to be meeting James and Hunter at Hunter's house. We couldn't find anybody to drop us off, so we decided to catch the bus. We must have been out of our minds. Neither one of us had on any boots, gloves, or hats, and we were wearing little skirts, trying to be cute and freezing our butts off. The bus ride was long as ever, but we must have waited about an hour for each bus in the dead of winter, and we took two busses and walked down about six streets to Hunter's house. We were so cold and hungry. When we got inside the house James and Hunter were acting strange, but I tried not to pay them any attention. I just wanted to warm up. We tried to get them to go to the corner and get us some McDonald's, but they kept saying

37

that they would go with us, but not without us. We started getting a little pissed off and got up to go to the restaurant. Alisha and I headed out the door before them, but we were in a hurry to get out of the cold that we didn't realize that they weren't behind us until we got there and found out that McDonald's had gone out of business. You see, they knew that and wanted to get rid of us, playing games. We saw the bus coming and ran after it to ride back home. That was the end of our west side journeys to see P.I.

19

The Restaurant Relationship

My first job in the Detroit, Michigan, area was at the Roseville Burger King. I was a cashier and I worked the grill. I tried to stay to myself, but of course that didn't happen. There was a girl named Michelle that had a twin sister and they worked with me. They were very loud and slutty. The manager that worked the morning shift was their cousin. I could never do anything right, and was always criticized. I had to work with her and her cousins until about 6 pm when the closing manager, Nate Powers, would relieve her. Nate was a funny Wesley-Snipes-type. I guess it wasn't hard to tell the relief I received when he took over the shift. He would come in and change my position, putting Michelle and Melba in the back to clean and work the grill. I would be on cash register and cleaning the lobby. When the night was over instead of me catching the bus, he would drop me off at home. We ended up becoming very close. I found out that I went to school with his baby sister, Nicole. We eventually began dating and no one but his mother was happy with our relationship. His sister was mad because I spent his money freely and drove his car and she couldn't even lean on it. At work the twins and their cousin kept trying to break us up.

One day that I was off work and the twins closed with Nate, Michelle got her wish. Their affair began. At this point he hadn't broken up with me. He hadn't even confessed to messing around with Michelle. So of course Michelle and her family couldn't wait to smack me in the face with it. Michelle started in telling me how she was prettier than I was and that her long hair and hips could get her anything she wanted. I kept telling her if she didn't have her hair she would be nothing more than a brown paper bag screw. Then she said, "I guess you'd have to ask Nate, since I screwed him and I'm pregnant with his baby." I was standing by the grill about to light it and when she said that I snapped and ended up setting her hair on fire. Without a question I was fired and Nate and I were through.

20

Senior Year

Everything about being a senior was so cool. I had a one to eight class schedule and I only had two required classes. We did so much together as a team. I actually didn't have a steady boyfriend. I ended up going to prom with Ricky, because he paid for everything, and his prom was the same week as mine was. I went with him to his prom, too. We weren't a couple, so after prom was over, I dropped him off at home.

During my senior year, I met Jericho Caesar. He worked at a collision shop around the corner from my house. Every week they used to gather at the shop to prepare for the street races. Deana, Kim, Connie, and I decided to walk to the store to get a little attention from the guys up at the shop.

As we were walking past the shop, I was on the inside, but didn't see him standing there. All I heard was, "Mmm! Mmm! Mmm!" So I responded, "Thank you!" All my girls started hollering. "What makes you think he was talking about you?" I asked them. "If you thought he was talking about you, you would have said thank you, too!" Well, mission accomplished; we turned the corner and headed back home, seeing the store wasn't on our agenda for real.

On the way back home, I was talking about not dealing with another guy who doesn't have transportation. I said the next guy that approaches me driving and not riding shotgun, I would give him my number. As soon as I got that out I my mouth, Jericho pulled up. He asked if he could talk to me. I started to give him the cold shoulder and then everyone reminded me of what I had just said. They ended up giving him my number.

Jericho and I grew really close. I found him very attractive because he was a single father of the cutest baby girl. Her name was Andrea. The love he had for his daughter was so beautiful. I remember that all of us used to go to Gibraltar Trade Center and everyone would ask me if she was my baby. I'd tell them no, but she's my God-Daughter. I tried to spoil her and get her the cutest little things. Jericho and I used to hang out together all the time, but never really anywhere that we would have to spend much money. We had become an obvious item.

Then his daughter's mother decided to come back into the picture. She was not happy that Jericho and I were together. She did everything she could think of to come between us, but one day I was at the collision shop with Jericho and she showed up. She started talking junk to me. The only thing that I recall is that she hit a nerve. Minnie was a Caucasian girl with a head full of curly hair. I recall her saying, "That's why your black man needs this white girl! See, you're going to have a problem keeping your man!" Then I remembered her throwing her arms around him and I walked off; I couldn't deal with all the drama. I ended up leaving Jericho alone. I always thought that what she said had to be true because he didn't come running after me. I was heartbroken. The next time I heard from him he wanted us to go out. I had set up plans to go out with someone else just to say I was preoccupied.

From that time in my life, I ended up just dating and not really being in a relationship with any one guy. I only wanted to be wined and dined.

21

Little Caesars

I needed extra money for my senior year: senior dues, hair-dos, school pictures, clothes, and a car. I applied at the pizza place and worked my schedule around school and cheerleading. It wasn't a great paying job, but it was better than being broke. I worked every weekend and every night, and I was really good at what I did. I was able to basically run the store alone but was constantly passed up for a promotion. I was upset about it, but this wasn't the career that I wanted to pursue so I tried not to let it get to me.

One day my school had planned a college tour with a job fair. I put in a month in advance to have that day off. I was promised by one of the managers doing the schedule that I would get it off, but when that weekend came for me to go, I was scheduled to work. I talked to the store manager and then the district manager, but no change came to the schedule. The day prior to my college tour and job fair I informed them that nothing had changed with the schedule, but I wasn't going to be here tomorrow. The shift manager told me, "If you don't come in tomorrow, then don't ever come back!" I shrugged it off and attended the college tour and job fair.

When I showed up for my schedule on Monday the district manager was there. He told me that I was fired for being insubordinate and a no-call no-show. I was hurt and angry and had no idea how I was going to pay for all my expenses. I went down to the unemployment office and filed for unemployment. They gave me an application that my former employer had to sign and document my wages. I took it that very same day back up to Little Caesars. The district manager was very arrogant. He signed the application and when I informed him that they needed documentation of my wages, he wrote, "See last check."

His arrogance ended up being a blessing, because my last check was the biggest I had ever received. I ended up receiving unemployment benefits for fifty-two weeks and my checks were more than I made on a regular week. I ended up making more money off work and fired than at work punching a clock!

22

Sick and Jealous

After graduation, I went right into a computer program at Focus Hope called Fast Trak. There I met Matthew Mills. We kicked it for a little bit, but broke up because his ex-girlfriend got pregnant by him while we were together. Matthew and I stopped communicating, but his mother, Monica, was so understanding. I remember her telling me that she was glad that her son and me didn't work out. It was like she could always see something more promising for me. Monica and I grew so close that she became the mother that I've always wanted and I was the daughter she never had.

After completing the program at Focus Hope, I proceeded to the National Education Center to get my Associates in Electronics Engineering Technology.

Towards the end of my high school years I became friends with Sharita Woods. She had sickle cell so she was always in and out of the hospital, but we still managed to hang out. This was around the time that I met Derek Hill.

He was a Japanese-Afro-American.

Derek and I hit it off almost immediately. It was funny because Derek and my cousin Deana tried to talk on the phone and there was no chemistry, so she kept giving me the phone. Derek and I got so close that I had access to all his bank accounts, credit cards, and home. I was invited over his house for dinner with his family, and his mother informed me that when Derek reached twenty-one, he would inherit $1.5 million dollars for being the first grandson on the Japanese side of his family. The only reason she told me was because Derek and I were talking about marriage and children.

Well, long story short, Sharita and Derek's best friend Richard were dating, and he had a fear of hospitals. Sharita was jealous of me and Derek's relationship so she told the most unbelievable lie. She had someone call Richard and tell him that she was dead. He became very upset and he and Derek called me on a three way. Richard was crying and I didn't know why. Derek started telling me that Sharita had passed. I said, "What?! Who told you that? I just got off the phone with her? Hold on! Let me call her in the hospital."

When I called, she answered the phone and I asked her what this was all about. She started laughing. I told her that this is not a joking matter and that Richard was very upset. When she found out that she was on three way, she lied on me. She said, "Don't act like you weren't in on it!" Derek started hollering and said, "Friends of a feather flock together, and if she'll lie like that, you will, too." He hung up and wouldn't return any of my phone calls. Then he came up to my job at Marianne's and told me that everything he ever gave me he wanted back or he was going to sue me for stealing. I was humiliated and angry; I gave everything back and I told Sharita if I ever saw her again I was going to let her know how it feels to hurt the way I did right then.

23

Becoming A Mommy

I graduated and continued to work at Marianne's. By this time, I had taken the test and passed in order to work for Michigan Bell. My cousin Deana was dating a Puerto Rican guy named Gerald who introduced me to his cousin, Edward Fisher. I thought he was so fine. We ended up messing around once and the second time, I got pregnant. He told me I was pregnant, but since I was on birth control pills, I didn't pay him any attention. After the second time, I left him alone, because I felt like he was trying to jeopardize my life, playing games with the condom.

Shortly after leaving Edward, I ran into Jericho. I had always had feelings for him, but our timing seemed to always be horrible. Ricky and I ended up getting an apartment together, because he wanted to make me happy. I gave in and tried to make it work. It was unbearable. I tried to break up with him, but he wouldn't let me. No matter what I said, he was still there. One day

I told him that I was leaving to find a real man and I'd be back Monday. He told me that if I wasn't back home tonight that all my stuff would be on the curb. That made me so happy.

I left and spent the weekend on the west side. It was 4th of July and I was drinking tequila and orange juice. I got so drunk that I went to lie down and didn't wake up for two days. I was so mad that no one tried to wake me up. I got up and left. When I made it back to the apartment, the house was clean and dinner was almost ready. All my clothes and personal items were still in their place. Ricky welcomed me home and wined and dined me. I was so upset.

I had been throwing up frequently, so I went to the doctor. I told him that I thought I might have alcohol poisoning. My physician took my blood and I waited patiently in the room. When he came back, he was laughing uncontrollably. He informed me that I didn't have alcohol poisoning, but I was almost four months pregnant. I sat there in disbelief. This couldn't be happening to me again. I couldn't get another abortion. I was upset because I utilized all the preventions and I was still pregnant. I rationalized that if I didn't have this baby the LORD wouldn't bless me with any children, and I wanted a child, just not now.

After I got a grip on the situation, I went with my best friend, Toya, over to southwest Detroit to locate Edward Fisher. When I found him and informed him that I was pregnant, he replied, "So, what do you want me to do? I'm going back to Puerto Rico."

I was devastated. If this wasn't déjà vu I didn't know what it was. That very moment I couldn't breathe or even focus. I jumped into my car and tried to run him down. All I remember is Toya hollering, "He ain't worth it, Yvonne!" I collected myself and threw my hands up in the air. I didn't need him to love my baby. We would be just fine.

24

A Man's Job

I was a twenty-year-old African-American female with an Associates of Science in Engineering Technology, and I was four months pregnant. My job with Michigan Bell, the local phone company, had only just begun. As soon as I found out about the baby, I informed my supervisor, Billy Newman. I had just completed all my training to obtain my position and he immediately attacked my character, accusing me of falsifying company records. He accused me of knowing I was pregnant and not disclosing this information. He told me, "If you are unable to do this job then you need to quit! I will not be making any exceptions for you!"

God blessed me to have two dispatchers, Gloria Little and Dorothy Butler, that felt my pain and they watched the work I received daily. My supervisor was still giving me jobs where I would have to lift and climb a 50-pound ladder. My dispatchers would take those jobs and give me something different that would be safer for me and my unborn child.

At this point my supervisor had become very ignorant. We would have meetings each morning before we began our routes and every day, he would put something unnecessary in my personal file, for example, "She sat at the meeting with a yellow pocket t-shirt on, rubbing her belly." After all the harassment and persecution, I went to the union and they began to build a case against him. I requested to be removed from his crew and he would tell me, "You don't have enough seniority to go anywhere. Be glad you have this job."

The union and I were recording conversations and taking notes. You see, Billy would say things to me and then say that he never said that, or I must have misunderstood him. I began to send letters to his boss and his boss's boss. I was inquiring if any transfers were available. Finally, I found out that there was a technician that was stationed in Downtown Detroit that wanted to come to Roseville where I was. I began calling his supervisor, Luke Thomas, and pestering him about transferring his tech to exchange with me. After about two weeks we were transferred on a verbal. This was the last transfer of this kind ever allowed, but it was already done. It was also told to me that they forced Billy Newman to retire because of the possibility of a discrimination lawsuit.

25

I Wanted Him

My son, Kevin Markice Williams, was only six months old and I used to take him everywhere I went. One day, my girlfriends and I got all dressed up and went to the Michigan State Fair. I was just getting over a break-up with Ricky. I went to Ce'la Vie, a designer clothing store, and brought a white and gold jean outfit to wear to the Fair. When we got there, it was so crowded and guys came from all over to talk to us. I was not in the mood for pick-up lines; I only wanted to have fun with my girls and be left alone.

We decided to ride the Pirate Ship. We stood in line and finally got up to the ride conductor. All I could concentrate on was him. He was sexy as all get down, clean cut with a hint of thug. I watched as all the girls drooled over him. When we finally got to the front of the line I asked him, "If I gave you my number, would you call me?" Without even looking at me he responded, "Yah!" His response seemed rehearsed I was instantly turned off. Still, I got on the ride and stared at him the whole time. After the ride, Alisha was trying to find paper and pencil to write my number down and give it to him. I kept telling her to forget it, but she snatched a piece of paper and eyeliner from some girl and wrote my number down for him.

While staying at Toya's I would forward my number there. Two weeks later, I got a call over Toya's house. I had no idea who the person was because friends of Toya would tell their friends to call me. I hated that. If I didn't give you my number, then you shouldn't be calling me. I answered the phone and he said, "Hello, can I speak to Yvonne?" I said, "Who's calling?" He replied, "Owen." I told him, "I don't know anyone named Owen! Who gave you my number?" He replied, very irritated, "You did! I met you at State Fair while I was working on the Pirate Ship." I instantly apologized and we talked for a little while before he invited me over his house. I told him I was taking my braids out and I was actually bald-headed and didn't want him to see me like this. He told me to put a hat on and come over and he would help me take them out. Of course I was lying about my hair. I just was trying to stall for time. I changed my clothes and met him over on Hampshire.

I put on my "Bongo" outfit. It was a cream button up bra with some short-shorts. My body was tight. I had brought myself a 1993 black-on-black in black four-door Dodge Shadow with chrome and black rims and tinted windows. I felt like I was all of that. When I finally made it to his house the whole block stopped to look. We sat on the porch and did a lot of talking. We ended up spending every day together. When he met Kevin, they hit it off great. Kevin didn't like many people, but he used to always fall asleep on Owen's chest. To me that did it. My son felt comfortable with him. He was in.

26

He Had A Dream

Owen and I spent every day from then together. When I was at work he kept Kevin for me. They became rather close. We ended up getting a place together. We moved on Horatio street in southwest Detroit. It was a two family flat and his mother stayed downstairs. I thought that would be cool, because all he talked about was his mother. We moved in and didn't have much furniture, but loads of clothes. Kevin had his own room with a crib and all his toys and we shared the other room. I made sure the house was always clean and we had plenty of food, even though it was a hole-in-the-wall type place. I wasn't happy to be there, but the idea of us being a family really made me happy.

I started to slowly notice things, like items out of the refrigerator missing when I planned on cooking them for dinner. I even noticed outfits that I couldn't find. Then one day Owen brought me a pair of gold hoop earrings. He always talked about me getting a second hole in my ear, so I did it. Well, I remember showing the earrings to his mother and she said to me, "Those are really nice! You know, if they come up missing, I got them." I laughed it off and didn't think much about it. A couple days later we came home and more food was missing, but this time my earrings and two of my Guess outfits were, too. I was puzzled because all the doors were locked as we left them. There wasn't a forced entry and we were the only two with keys.

Owen ran downstairs to his mother. All I could hear was a lot of fussing and hollering. When Owen came back he told me that he would get me some more outfits and another pair of earrings. I started in asking him what happened to my stuff. Just then his mother came upstairs and was explaining that she used a screwdriver to slip the lock and her boyfriend and her had been eating the steaks, and she needed a fix, so she sold my outfits and earrings. I couldn't believe my ears. I lunged at her and Owen jumped in between us. I had no idea his mother was a crackhead; I was so out done. Then, I found out that she had been smoking up the rent we had been paying—so much so that we were being evicted. I didn't like the idea of renting in the first place, so I started looking for a house to purchase. I promised him that his mother would not be allowed to even step foot into our house.

We ended up viewing several houses and I didn't fall in love with any of them, but the agent kept trying to get me to look at this brick bungalow on a corner lot. The resident was just removed and placed into a senior apartment. The house was a mess. The agent was convinced that I would love it, so he scheduled for us to see it after it was painted and cleaned up. The price was good and the neighborhood was quiet. Upon our second visit I was really impressed, then he took us upstairs and this is where I fell in love. The master bedroom was upstairs and had walls of knotted pine paneling. It had three closets and one was a walk-in. There were drawers built right into the wall and a bookshelf at the stairway.

"You have a deal!" I told the real estate agent. We moved in and furnished the house with everything brand new from Art Van Furniture.

After getting situated we got engaged. We planned to have at least a year engagement, but things didn't work out like that. In the midst of planning the wedding, I found out I was pregnant, so all our plans had to be moved up six months. I had already purchased my wedding gown and I was unable to get a refund on it and I was determined to wear it. We ended up getting married December 23, 1995. Mr. And Mrs. Koby Owen Jones; I was four months pregnant. The wedding, the reception, and the honeymoon were a blur. I settled and compromised to please everybody but myself. It didn't feel like it was my wedding at all.

After everything was back to normal, Koby started having dreams. He kept hollering, "Kenneth! Kenneth!" One night, I woke him to see what the problem was. He was in a cold sweat and hyperventilating.

"I can't find him! I can't find him! He's lost!" Koby said. "Who is lost?" I inquired. "KENNETH!" he shouted. "Who is Kenneth?" I asked him. He looked at me as if he couldn't believe I was asking him such a question, and replied, "Kenneth is our son!" I was speechless seeing that I was still pregnant and still had a couple months to go.

27

Earning Respect

I was so glad to be in Detroit at the Abbott Street Garage instead of out at the Ten Mile Garage in Roseville. The first problem I encountered was that Owen was the son of William Peter Jones, who was an AT&T technician, too, out of the Linwood garage. His reputation preceded him as a lazy and worthless worker. Since Koby Owen Jones and I were engaged to be married, Kyle Cook, another technician in my crew tried to attach William's reputation to me, saying, "Oh, boy, another Jones!" in a way that meant I was worthless, too. I took his smart comments for so long that one day I just went off. I told him my name is Yvonne, not William, and you can't judge me for his reputation, because I am not him. Kyle started getting loud, telling me, "You had better respect your elders!" I replied, "You have to give respect to get respect, and as far as you and I, we are co-workers. Your age means nothing to me, but you've had a lot longer to be stupid." After that, Kyle and I never really had any other words and he left me alone.

I made a whole bunch of friends at my job, but I also made an enemy, Paula Woods. I have been told that she used to turn heads in her younger years, but between now and then she must have had some hard times. She actually lived in the same direction that I did, and she needed a ride home. I had no problem giving her a ride, but the problem came when Owen and I had an argument and she was in the car. She went back to work and told all my business and began to call me out insulting me, and then she had the nerve to have an attitude with me. She was just out of control. So instead of arguing with her or even fighting her, I ignored her. I could walk past her and not even notice she was there. I could have a conversation with someone on the other side of her and never make any eye contact. She became invisible to me.

28

My Baby Boy

Koby and I had been engaged for about a year. We planned on having a summer wedding, but it was changed to two days before Christmas. So, on June 3, 1996, Kenneth Owen Jones was born.

I remember Koby was at work and he gave me a call. I was cleaning house but every five to seven minutes, I would put him on hold. After about the sixth time, he asked me what I was doing. I told him that I must have gas because my side kept hurting. We talked about another twenty minutes and in that time, he was monitoring each time I put him on hold. Finally, he told me that I might be in labor and should call my doctor. I did and my doctor said told I was in labor and about to have that baby at home. He told me I needed to get to the hospital. I was floored. I had Kevin two years earlier and my labor pains were much worse.

I called Koby back and he promised to be there before I delivered, but he was at work forty-five minutes away. I was home with Kevin and didn't want him to go to the hospital with me. Kevin was always so upset when I seemed to be in pain. I called everybody, but the only person that was available was Aunt Rita who didn't have a car. So I got Kevin and I into the Jeep and headed to grandma's house to pick up Aunt Rita.

The lights were timed perfectly. At every red light I had a contraction and when the light changed it was over. After we made it to Aunt Rita's, she took me to the hospital. I believe the longest part of the delivery was the insurance paperwork and the same questions by four different people. I started hollering, "Don't ask me another question. Talk to the first person I talked to."

At that point Koby ran in. He made it to the hospital in less than twenty minutes. The nurse finally examined me and moved me to labor and delivery. My doctor came in and said I wasn't quite ready and to page him when I was. Ten minutes later I was ready for delivery, but the doctor was nowhere to be found. They didn't want me to push but my contractions were getting closer and closer. Finally the doctor showed up and with three pushes Kenneth was born. I knew from his first few minutes that he would be a fighter and a loud mouthed individual. He laid in the incubator quiet while he wasn't being messed with, but as soon as someone touched him, he began to holler. The only person he didn't holler at when they touched him was Koby. They looked so much alike it was scary.

29

I Didn't Want This

I remember when the change began. Koby had just had his 21st birthday. He came to me and told me, "I am ready to be the man I've always wanted to be." I inquired what that was. He told me, "All this time I have been doing the things that you wanted to do. I have been going places that you wanted to go. I am ready to be my own man." Shortly after that he started hanging out with the wrong crowd. He started lying about not smoking. He started disappearing for long periods of time then reappearing with expensive items.

Koby and I were rapidly growing apart. He wanted the glitter and glamour of the streets. I was working hard for everything I had and trying to obtain a degree at the same time. We did a lot of separating and getting back together, but in the midst of it all my marriage became abusive.

One time while Koby and I were separated, our son Kenneth was having his first birthday and I wanted him to have a gift from Mommy and Daddy. I went and picked

Koby up, and knowing that he didn't have any money, I got into the passenger seat and told him let's go out to Fairlane Mall to find Kenneth a birthday gift. I could tell he wasn't happy about not having anything to offer, but I took it in stride. When we got to the mall he was so uncooperative that I decided to pick an outfit from the Guess store. The moment I opened my purse to pay for the outfit he started acting really strange. He started hollering, "I know that you aren't spending another man's money on my son!" I looked at him like he was crazy and replied, "This is my money. I do have a job, you know!"

He was so convinced that the money that I was spending came from someone else, that he started to argue with me in the mall. I was so embarrassed that I was just ready to leave. We made it back to car and Koby drove. He did a lot of fussing, but I let him rant and rave. We made it to the exit before my house and he pulled over on the shoulder on the freeway.

I looked at him and he said, "Every time I look at you, I think of a whore, and do you know what they do to whores? They beat them!"

At that moment he started hitting me in my face open handed. I was in shock at first, but when I came back to reality I put my hands up to stop the blows. I had blood everywhere. My kids were sitting in the backseat looking scared. I grabbed a diaper out of the diaper bag and wiped up the blood. Koby put the car into gear and told me that he was heading to my house so that I could call the police on him. My mind told me that if he would do this to me in public than it was no telling what would happen when I made it home behind closed doors. I looked back at my babies and said a silent prayer for their safety.

As we approached the light, I jumped out. Koby tore the bottom half of my shirt off me when I ran to the gas station for help. Koby did a U-turn and tried to hit me with my own car. I made it into the gas station and the owner hid me in the back room and let me get myself together.

I eventually called a friend of mine named Antwan. He instructed me to call my best friend Toya and have her bring me to his house where he would meet us. I called my grandmother and had my cousin Derek get my car and my kids.

That evening the kids and I stayed over Antwan's house. I felt so safe with him. We ended up staying there for a little while. Antwan was a great guy. He was in the Army, and was very neat, clean, organized and very disciplined. Antwan and I grew very close, but we had two problems; I was still married and his mother. His mother is one of those women that raises her son to be the man that she always wanted and at some point, gets confused at her role in his life. The straw that broke the camel's back was when we went to see Antwan at his parent's house, but his mother was no longer living there. As we walked into the door she put on her fake smile and greeted us. My kids and I spoke, but she wanted my kids to run and hug her. My son asked me if he had to. I told him no, but you do have to speak. She got mad and went into the kitchen where Antwan was cooking and told him, "If Yvonne had raised them children correctly she would have made them respect me!!"

Then she started talking about me being a bad mother. Instead of Antwan checking his mother's behavior, he came in the living room and began to chastise me about how I raised my kids. I have never had anybody say anything bad about my kids, because all I hear is how well-behaved they are and how great their manners are. I snapped, I told him if his mother had a man and hadn't raised him to be the man she always wanted then she wouldn't be so pressed with my kids not wanting to deal with her fake self. And if he was coming out here to teach me a lesson about my kids, then we were leaving. That incident terminated any relationship that we could have had.

30

Love in the Workplace

We ended up getting a new guy in our crew at work. He was somewhat interesting because everyone else in my crew was old enough to be my father. His name was Darnell White. He had just graduated from Howard with a degree in Engineering. It was kind of cool because he was able to assist me with my schoolwork since I was working and going to school. We ended up spending all day together at work as well as doing our routes together. We were very unaware of the trouble we were getting into, but MY HEAVENLY FATHER sent one of his angels to assist and protect me.

For about a year, this went on every workday. He began to look for a house and because of my feelings for him, I helped him with locating and decorating this house. We were definitely moving closer together each day. Well, I can't remember what holiday it was, but he told me that his family was going on a trip and he would be gone for about a week and he'd call me every day.

My days went on but I missed him so much. The day he returned, I was running late for work so when I saw him, he was talking to another one of our co-workers. Everybody knew about Darnell and I. Darnell's back was turned to me and I was getting closer and the coworker was looking dead at me. He asked Darnell, "So how was your HONEYMOON?"

I couldn't believe my ears when Darnell started giving all the details of Niagara Falls. I was speechless. I pushed him out of my way and headed into the office to pick up my work. He ran after me and I refused to speak or even look at him. I treated him as if he never existed. He jumped up and down having fits, but I left and cried the whole day. I found out that everyone at work but me knew about him getting married. I felt so stupid and humiliated. I had to continue to work in the same crew with him and everybody thought that I was some kind of tramp.

He eventually got promoted to Engineering and I refused any contact with him from that time on. After the relationship that we had, I refused to be in that kind of situation again, especially with a guy that I work with. Since I worked with over sixty guys, it actually made a lot of people angry at him for messing it up for someone else.

31

Pulling It Back Together

We got back into our daily routines. My youngest son Kenneth started missing his father and wanted to see him so I started going out of my way to make that possible. I started going by his grandmother's house and trying to communicate with him. I found out that he was living with some young chick with three or four kids and on government assistance. My children tried to spend time with him, but the only time they did, was when he stopped by my house.

My husband and I did a lot of talking and decided to try to make our marriage work. I went over to his grandmother's house and his girlfriend was there. I sat down and talked to her and tried to find out if he had promised her anything or was he responsible for anything at her house. I wanted to know if she was pregnant. We came to an understanding and she agreed that if we were still married that their relationship had to end. I let her know that he was coming back home and we started over.

His ex-girlfriend started calling him and begging him to come back. He would always give me the phone after telling her not to call back and that it was over. When I got the phone, we talked and she was just as understanding as she was before. I was trying to be patient with her because of the situation and I knew that she had her feelings involved. Then she blurted out, "I'm pregnant! And I need to talk to him about it."

I hit the ceiling and threw the phone out of the window to him. The next thing that I remember is he and his friend got into the car and pulled off. My mother was on her way over so as soon as she got to the house, I headed over to his ex-girlfriend's house. As I was driving towards her house, Koby and his friend were coming back and saw me flying up the street. I made it to the house and grabbed my keys. I jumped out of my Jeep and walked towards her and some guy on her front porch. My whole intent was to talk to her, but the first thing out of her mouth was, "Now!"

I grabbed her by her throat and slung her into the bushes and started punching her in the face, telling her, "I thought I told you not to inconvenience my life. I told you that I wasn't going to deal with you being pregnant."

Koby and Jimmy pulled up and pulled me off her. She got up and said, "So! I'm keeping it!"

I broke free and started kicking and stomping her. Koby picked me up and put me into the Jeep. She was still talking junk to me. I put my Jeep into gear and tried to run her down, but with no avail.

After making it home and calming down I felt horrible. I always said I'd never fight over any guy, but in my mind it was a respect thing and not over Koby. The very next morning I called her and apologized and offered my assistance. She declined my help but I never really lived down the guilt.

32

Improving Myself

I had been attending Wayne State University since 1993, but only taking one class every other semester. I was introduced to the National Society of Black Engineers. I always wanted to be a part of a sorority, but I never wanted to go online and degrade myself just to hang out with them. This organization offered everything the sororities offered, but no hazing and I would be in contact with other students taking the same classes and also the alumni already in my field of study.

I was very excited to be a part of this international organization. We had several conferences per year. In these conferences we had huge job fairs with all the big names in engineering there. There were workshops that coached professional conduct and workshops that assisted you with resume writing. I loved the fact that we had conferences all over the world, which gave me a chance to see other states at a reasonable rate.

The Wayne State chapter was also affiliated with The

Association of Black Engineers and Applied Science. We had weekly meetings and had an executive board. After being a member for about one year I was elected Program Coordinator. I had so many ideas of events we could have or sponsor.

One night in October, we were having a bowling night. I was so excited that I could bring my family to meet my NSBE family. Of course, my husband was nonchalant and anti-social. He initially didn't want to go, so I invited my younger cousin, Alona, to go with me. But at the last minute he changed his mind.

When we got there, I was the first female to show and there where fifteen guys already there. I felt a lot of tension coming from my husband, so I instantly tried to offset the pressure. Everybody we met, I introduced him as my husband, and they welcomed him, but he was a tough guy and didn't want to be bothered. The president of our chapter, Allan April, came and tried to lighten the mood, but Koby didn't want to be bothered by anyone. So my cousin and I jumped up and got in the next game. He jumped up and wanted the keys to the Jeep so he could come back and get us. By him insisting to come and the bowling alley was on the other side of town, I told him, "No, but just have a seat we're only playing a few games." He sat there and mean-mugged everyone the whole time.

After the last game was over I said my goodbyes and we headed home. All the way home he sat looking out the window. Alona and I did a little talking and a lot of singing. When Alona had made it home we said our goodbyes. Upon approaching my block, Koby jumped out of the Jeep while it was still rolling. All I could think about was, "NOT AGAIN!"

I didn't feel like arguing or fighting, and I could tell that it would be one or the other. He started hollering and screaming, "You have got to be kidding me! I know that you are messing around with one of those guys and you just want me to be stupid!"

I told him that I wasn't and asked him to get back in the Jeep. He just kept hollering and telling me that he couldn't trust me. At that point I put the Jeep into park and reached over and closed the passenger door. I put the Jeep into drive and pulled off. I ended up driving down to Chandler Park and sitting for a while. I remember looking at him. I could see in his eyes he was on something different. I knew that he was going through some things with the loss of his grandmother, who basically grounded him. I went back home to see if he had calmed down and if he wanted to talk.

When I pulled up to the house he was sitting on the porch and his eyes were red. I cracked the window and asked him if he needed to get some air, and maybe go somewhere or wanted someone to pick him up. He walked closer to the Jeep and he was crying, "All I want is you to love me. I want my wife!"

He stood outside of the Jeep and talked to me through the window. I let the window down a little to hand him some tissue, but I was still nervous about him. As I cracked the window, he used both of his hands and tried to force it down. I started hollering and screaming, "STOP IT!!" I put the Jeep into gear to pull off and he grabbed me by the neck with both hands and started choking me and screaming, "DIE!" I swerved and accelerated trying to get him to let my neck go. I was blowing my horn and burning rubber and no one came to my aid. I ended up making it to the main street and he climbed up on the hood and held onto the rack and kicked my windshield until it shattered.

Now, the police showed up. He started telling them that I was trying to kill him. He wanted to hurt me some sort of way and he knew that the insurance had lapsed and I had no way of getting it fixed. I got out and started screaming, "I knew marrying you was a mistake. You are the biggest loser I've ever known. You will never amount to anything. My mother was right. You are a burden and will do nothing but hold me back. I hate you!"

The police tried to calm me down to find out if I wanted him to go to jail. I knew that if he went to jail that night that he would definitely miss his grandmother's funeral. I knew that if he missed her funeral I might as well relocate. I asked them to call his father to have him come and get him to talk to him or something. When I got on the phone with him he asked me, "What did you want me to do with him? I'm sleeping." I knew at that moment that I had no help from his family.

33

Thanks for Being There

We were at a conference with National Society of Black Engineers and having the time of our lives. Imagine having a hotel party that extended across four hotels and on every floor it was a party. Meka, Evaline and I had just come back from swimming. Everyone came up to our room to play cards; everyone in our room was from our school except two guys.

The phone kept ringing left and right. Meka and Evaline ended up leaving and promising to come right back. Slowly the room began to empty. The two guys and Lawrence and I were still playing our last hand of spades. When the game was over, the other two guys started acting strange. I began cleaning up, hinting for them to leave, but they wanted to stay and I began to feel a little uneasy.

Lawrence started packing up his things. I grabbed him into the bathroom and begged him not to leave me. I felt they were going to try to rape me or try something against my will. He told me he had the same idea and he wouldn't dare leave me like that. I reached up and hugged him and I just couldn't let go. The other guys hollered into the bathroom door, "Hey! Dog! Why don't you save some for us!"

Lawrence hollered back, "Naw! Dog! I'm not sharing. We'll holler at y'all later. Close the door behind you!"

They ended up leaving. I told everyone how if Lawrence Summers wasn't there I might have been a statistic. He ended up being my secret admirer and we kicked it on the down-low. Our relationship ended because of my stupid estranged husband who tried to scare any man away from me.

34

Having a Heart

By this time in my life I had lost a whole bunch of respect from my friends and family. No one could understand why I was going through what Koby was taking me through and why was I still accepting him back into me and my kid's lives. Koby and I had been separated for a little while when his sister had her baby and was living with me. Koby would come by from time to time to see the kids. Every time I saw him, he looked worse.

He had gotten into the habit of asking me for a sandwich because he was hungry. I have never been a cold-hearted person so it started to weigh on my heart. This is the father of my children. I just couldn't see him on his knuckle like this. I knew it was a long-shot, but I extended a proposal: "If you get a job or go to school I will help you get back on your feet. I will help you get to where you need to and get you the needed clothing, and when you can fend on your own you will repay me."

We had an agreement. He moved into the basement and I kept up my end of the bargain. Koby started attending business school and returned to work at Oakland Mall. I felt really good about everything. I knew that he had it in him. He was always intelligent. When he tested for his placement, he was at the top in scores. It was an eighteen-month course and upon completion they would place him in a position. I could actually see him making something of himself.

Well one day Tiffany, Connie and I went shopping. Before leaving the city I called Koby to let him know that my cell phone battery was low and I was going shopping and I would talk to him later. This was just out of common courtesy. While we were out my cell phone rang then died. I didn't think anything about it. I figured I had my kids with me and Koby knows we are shopping, so anyone else can just leave a message.

Upon arriving home saw Koby sitting on the porch. I could tell he was having a problem, but at the time my kids were hungry and needed to be fed. Koby met us at the garage and demanded, "We need to talk!"

I told him okay, but my kids need to eat first. You will have to wait a minute. He wasn't happy with my answer and it was very obvious the way he stomped around. I just kept thinking to myself, I hope he ain't on no dumb stuff, because I don't have the patience for it today.

After I placed the food onto my kid's plates he snatched me out the front door to the porch. I was very heated at this point and felt the disrespect in his gestures. He started in, "I called you several times and all I got was voicemail. Where were you? Why was you avoiding my calls? What took you so long to make it back home? Who was with you?"

I replied, "First of all, don't step to me like I owe you anything. You are not my man! You don't have a right to be all in my face like this! And on that note, I don't have to stand here and have you interrogate me!"

I turned to go back into the house. He snatched my keys, locked the door, and threw my keys. He told me, "You are going to stand there and listen to whatever I say."

I walked off the porch he started choking me. I bit his arm to make him stop, but instead he bit me under my arm. I couldn't believe this was happening. We fought out in front of my house. His sister was on the phone with her son's father and he was on his way to get them. I ended up getting back into the house and started calling the police. He snatched the phone out of the wall and went through the house snatching all the other phones out. He told me that wasn't nobody coming to help me. I grabbed my cellphone and called 911, but my battery didn't last. His sister left out the side door to get help and her son's father pulled up. Koby threatened them so they left to get help. I locked all the doors and set the alarm off so that the police would know that I needed help.

I took my kids into their room and told them to stay put and stay quiet and that the police would be there really soon.

Since my keys were outside, Koby had access to my house. He walked into the door with an axe in his hands. I ran out of the house and headed down the street. He ran after me and dragged me back to the house by my hair. I felt so helpless. I didn't want to leave my kids, but I need to flee for my safety. I prayed for my kids' safety and made a break for it again. He dragged me back kicking, biting and screaming. At this point I was sitting on the porch without my shirt or bra on and crying. A Jeep pulled up and two guys got out. They asked me if I was okay. I was so mad that I was sarcastic. "Do I look alright?" Then Koby came to the door with the axe in his hand. He started threatening the guys, thinking I called them for help. They looked at me and said, "It'll be o.k." The guy on the porch reached into his shirt and pulled out his badge and demanded, "DETROIT POLICE! STEP OUT OF THE HOUSE!"

I couldn't believe it. They were undercover police! They put him in handcuffs and gave me my keys. They had me go and cover myself, but they had to take pictures first of all my bruises. You will not believe that while all of this was going on, no one came out to stop it or assist me, but when he was on the ground and in handcuffs the whole neighborhood was out.

After that ordeal was over, I finalized our divorce on January 7, 1999. We'd never go through this again. I began to pursue getting my CCW and made it clear to him that I am not the woman you used to know. Try me!

35

The Vision of My Poetry

With the divorce I got it all, because Koby didn't show up for the divorce hearing. I had a Jeep and an Impala, both with car notes, a house with a house note, and the credit card debt from eleven maxed cards. Plus two kids to take care of. I needed help with the Impala, it had been stolen and the insurance company denied the claim. I was slowly putting my life back together.

I encountered the Impala Car Club at Belle Isle one day and decided to give them a call and see what they were all about. I ended up playing phone tag with one of the Vice Presidents of the club. We ended up scheduling a meeting so they could take a look at my car. I was kind of swept away with Kurt the Vice President that I had been playing phone tag with. He seemed very intelligent and business-minded. I was a little leery about inviting them to my house, so we met at a park nearby and I brought my kids plus two of my girls, Alisha and Lavern to meet with Karl (President), Dale (Vice President) and Kurt (Vice

President). When I first saw Kurt I thought he had it going on and he was very attractive. I had made up in my mind that I wanted him. So I began flirting. We ended up making plans to have him come by tomorrow and fix on my car.

When he arrived he worked so diligently on cleaning and shining my car. After a couple hours he asked if he could get me and the kids something to eat since he had to go up the street to the auto parts store. The kids had been playing with him since yesterday and I could tell they were really fond of him. When we got to KFC and was in the lobby ordering, they were playing a name-calling game and Kevin, my oldest son, got carried away and called Kurt a bastard. My mouth hit the floor. I snatched him out of the store and I wore him out in the car. I apologized to Kurt and so did Kevin. I knew for a fact that he was done with me. Who wants to deal with a woman who has unruly children?

Well, we headed back to my house and he spent a little more time with us. The Impala Car Club had meetings on Saturdays. Kurt called me to remind me to attend. I told him I was rather nervous, but I would be there.

The day of the meeting I called Lavern to have her go with me. When we arrived, Kurt introduced me to everybody. We did a ride out from Evergreen and Grand River to Jefferson and Grand Blvd at Belle Isle. I had so much fun. I was named The First Lady I.P.P. The guys always tried to test my driving skills. The very first time they got on I-96 and everyone hit 80-100 miles an hour. They didn't expect me to keep up. I had to show them that I was a rider, too, even though I am a female.

Well, after a few club meetings, Kurt and I had become really close, but he insisted that we didn't let the club know that we were dating. He felt that they would take it as a conflict of interest. I didn't like it but I went along with it anyway.

36

Meeting My Father and Family

In the beginning of December, 2001, I had come to the point in my life that family meant everything to me, but I felt like the outcast or the black sheep of my family. Kurt and I were talking about marriage, contemplating relocating to Las Vegas, Nevada where he lived before he met his ex-wife. We had begun planning a trip for the beginning of the year.

I seemed to always be down in spirit when the holidays came around. You would think I didn't have any family or they all lived in another state, but in actuality the majority of my family stayed within a ten to fifteen minute drive, and no one hardly ever came to visit or check up on me.

Well, this Christmas, I felt like it was time for my family to hear and understand how I was feeling. For all my aunts, cousins and of course my grandmother, I typed each of them a very personal note of how I appreciated what they had done for me and I expressed my thankfulness. I concluded each with a farewell and have a good life. I resented that if I was going to live here in Detroit and be without family and their love then it was pretty much a no brainer to leave and start a new beginning in Las Vegas.

I didn't want anyone to label me as ungrateful. I was very thankful for all the things that each individual had done for me, but this was nothing like what I pictured a family being or feeling like. I felt more in the family with Kurt's family. They welcomed me in with open arms, and it wasn't just because I was Kurt's girlfriend. They called me, "Auntie Vonn," and still do.

Upon completing the cards and dropping them in the mail, I thought about my father. He lived about five minutes away. I was still angry with him, I was twenty-eight years old, and my paternity had still not been established. My mother always told me he was my father and after meeting up with him a few times, I had no doubt in my mind. I had approached him several times with the approval of a DNA test. I even told him that I would pay for it, but he always refused. So along with the other Christmas cards, I dropped one in the mail for him as well. I informed him that I was disappointed in him, and I couldn't understand how he could sleep at night knowing that he has a daughter that he has never been a part of her life. I told him that most men want a son, and grandfathers want grandsons. I told him that he has two that he has never even attempted to lay eyes on. I told him that he'd be responsible that I'd never know how it feels to know that I possibly have sisters in the same city that I live in and we have never met and probably will never meet. I gave him a farewell and informed him I was relocating to Las Vegas and he wouldn't have to ever worry about me writing or trying to contact ever again. Inside the card I included our latest family picture.

Two days later, I came home and found a note on my front door. It said, "I got your card. Call me!" and there was a number attached. I instantly got scared and began to question my fears, "What if I meet with him and we do a DNA test and he isn't my father? What if I know some of my sisters and we have already met on unpleasant grounds?"

I decided to give him a call. We met and talked and he tried to explain his side of the story. I pretty much was uninterested in any conversation without a DNA test. I called and scheduled an appointment. I charged the $750.00 on my credit card and held on tight for I knew this was going to be a wild ride. Needless to say the resolute came out 99.99% sure that Nicholas Green is my father. It brought an instant calm over my soul. I was able to finally stop searching for who I was and imagining what the other part of my family is like.

My father wasted no time getting my five sisters (Kate, Leah, Tara, Tess and Debbie) and I together. After all these years, I was worried how they would receive me. My father started bragging about me. He may have just been trying to inform them about me, but from one woman to another that was bragging and he was putting me on a pedestal, and that instantly incited jealousy. I wanted so much for our relationship to last, so I humbled myself and kept quiet.

I ended up spending a lot of time with my older sister Kate. She seemed really cool and down to earth. We started exercising together, emailing each other and keeping in touch daily. Kate was the sister that everybody was cool with. Even though all of us were sisters, each of us had a different mother, so of course we had a host of different personalities. Tess and I were a few months apart and when I looked at her she favored my mother. Leah was my older sister just above Tess. Leah was very possessive about our father. It was always, "MY DADDY!" Tara was the sister that didn't have anything to do with the family. She was still angry of the way she was brought up and our father didn't help or see about her. She had grown up in foster care instead of with our father. My baby sister Debbie is my favorite sister. She wasn't able to be at the original meeting, but she loved me just the same. She was so thrilled to have another older sister, with the chance that this sister would be cool and down to earth and accept her with love. Debbie and I called and talked all the time. She was in her senior year of high school and was about to leave for Chicago to attend college there. She showed me the most love out of that whole family.

One day, Kate was having a barbecue at her house and I was invited. When Kurt and I arrived, we met her husband and a few more cousins. The atmosphere was okay, I guess. The weather was nice and I dressed to impress. I wore my mint green DKNY capri outfit and accented it with baby pink shoes and jewelry. The evening was cool; at least I thought it went over rather well. A couple of days later I received a call from my older sister, Tara. She started in with, was I having any problems with any of my other sisters. I told her no and that it really felt good. Then she replied, "I was just on the phone with Kate and Tess. Kate feels like you were trying to seduce her husband." I was dumbfounded. "Why and when did I even have a chance to even spend any time with her husband?" I asked myself.

Tara went on to tell me that Kate and Tess said I looked like a whore, because I wore a thong with my capris and they couldn't see a panty line. At this point, I had enough of the he-said she-said. I got off the phone with Tara and immediately called Kate and Tess, but of course neither was available to answer their phone. I left a message for them to get back with me as soon as possible. When I got online, Kate was online too, so I instant-messaged her. Then she emailed me a letter. She wanted to know who told me that. I refused to drop names, but explained that it doesn't matter who said what to me. I am coming to you as a woman, not a gossiping teenager. She did a whole lot of name-calling and loud talking. After I realized that this conversation was going nowhere, I ended it.

I called Tara back to let her know how everything went down, but she refused to talk with me, too. A couple of days went by and I had received a couple childish emails from Kate. I ended up emailing her back and telling her that maybe if she wasn't having insecurity problems or troubles keeping her man's attention with those 2-XL bloomers on, she would be able to see that I was totally out of her husband's league, and she had no worries of him ever being my type. Not even in his best wet dream, but of all things, I deserved the benefit of the doubt since we were sisters. It just really offended me that she felt I wasn't trustworthy and for no fault of my own. After sending that email, I blocked her from sending me any further emails.

My sister Leah tried several times to help mend our relationship, but as usual, Kate refused to budge. I pretty much discontinued contact with all of them except for Debbie.

The next time that the six of us were in the same place was for my father's 60th birthday. It took a whole lot for me to even attend, but I mustered the energy out of respect for my father.

When I arrived, I had an uneasy feeling, and just as I expected, I was the outsider. They formed a clique and I wasn't a member. I remember my sister Kate speaking to my children and greeting them, but walking right past me as if I wasn't standing in front of her. When my baby sister arrived, I was ready to leave, but I stuck around for her. I took it upon myself to speak and try to have a conversation with them, but to no avail. We ended up taking a picture that my father wanted of all his children and himself. I went right to the back and stood next to my baby sister, but my father called me up to sit next to him on his right side. It was obvious that the jealousy and envy was very high in that room.

When we finished, I said my goodbyes and my kids and I left. This was the last time we were all together.

37

Blinders Off

Kurt used to live off Fenkell and Lasher with his nephew, because he was going through a divorce. I recall one day he called me to tell me that his Impala was being repossessed. He was highly upset and I was dumbfounded, because I gave him the car note money out of my savings account. (This was around the time that my best friend Toya and I stopped communicating. Well, maybe I should say She stopped talking to me or even receiving any of my calls. I found out later it was because of him.)

I later found out that he hadn't been paying the car note and the car was in his name with his ex-wife as the co-signer. Shortly after the car repo, he moved in with my kids and I, and since I had a Jeep and the Impala, I let him drive my car until he got his business straightened out. I was so proud to have a man like him. He told me he used to be a Michigan State Policeman, but relocated to Las Vegas Nevada and was on the Las Vegas Police Department there. He was also a sales representative for

Sprint. He told me that when he and his ex-wife met, he fell completely in love and sold everything to move back to Detroit. They ended up having a very short marriage and he told me it was because they didn't know each other well.

We would also be together for the holidays. I met all his family and they made me feel like one of the family. By this time, my nose was so wide open, that Kurt could have told me he was going to the moon for a couple months and he needed me pack his bags and I would have probably said, " Okay, baby, just be careful and call me." I thought that my prayers and all my dreams that I write poems about, had been answered. That was so far from the truth.

Scott Max Snowden, a.k.a. Kurt, was and is a great liar. You know the saying Game Peeps Game? Well, I didn't peep any of it. I have never met such an untrustworthy and disloyal individual.

I helped Kurt get a job for Pepsi as a merchandiser, so needless to say, his schedule was really flexible. I started to notice that he would smell different and he'd say it was something he tried at work. He would get pages in the middle of the night and wouldn't answer them, he'd say, "I am with my woman! Nothing else matters right now." We would go over his family's house for the holiday and he would always need to make a run the store only to come back hours later. There were so many things that sent up red flags that I totally ignored because I thought he was the man I'd been wanting all my life.

One day the Impala club met around the corner from my house at one of the member's sister's house. By this time, everybody knew about Kurt and me. When we walked into the door and the member was introducing everyone to his sister, her daughter ran up to Kurt and hugged him. I looked like, "Oh! You know them already." He told me, "No, I guess she can tell I'm a good person. You know kids are a good judge of character."

It didn't sit right with me but I let it go. A couple of weeks later I was coming home from school and just so happened to be driving down Chandler Park Drive. I saw my car at the sister's house. I got very angry. I circled back to get a look at the license plate. Sure enough it was my car. I pulled to the corner and walked towards the house. Kurt had come out and he pulled behind my Jeep and came running after me. He started explaining that he was just sitting in front of her house to see how much I trusted him. I was crying and angry. I tried to swing on him and then go to her house and give her a piece of my mind, too.

All I remembered was him picking me up kicking and screaming. I eventually stopped, because this wasn't like me. He went on explaining and apologizing. I told him, "At this point he was no better than my ex-husband. He abused me physically and you are trying to mess with my mind!"

He cried and begged and pleaded. He told me he would never hurt me. I told him we were through, but of course when it all boiled down, I gave him another chance. I hadn't caught him in a lie before so I wiped the slate clean and started over in my mind.

Everything seemed great again, then his pager and phone started going off in the middle of the night. I questioned him, but of course he avoided the topic and tried to sweet talk his way out of it. So when he went to sleep I checked his voicemails. The first message was from his nephew's ex-girlfriend. Her message was, "I just wanted to tell you I really enjoyed myself last night!" The second message was the sister around the corner. She revealed, "I've been missing you! Call me!" The third message was from a latchkey teacher from my kid's school. She wanted him to know that she'd be at her mother's house about that time.

I was furious so I deleted the messages. His defense was he didn't get any messages. He told me that he communicates with women, but there is nothing wrong with talking. So I went, okay, if he is going to do that, I can do it, too. But that wasn't in me. I felt so disappointed with myself for ignoring the signs. I didn't know what to think if I had labeled him the guy of my dreams. Maybe I didn't really know what I wanted and I decided to gradually take my heart back and get rid of him. We had no trust and I had no respect for him.

The straw that broke the camel's back was when I saw him with a new pager and new cell phone and I didn't have the numbers.

We went to church that Sunday and Kurt wasn't himself. The pastor was talking about everything going on in our lives and he didn't want to hear it. When we made it home, he went to the basement and turned on the football game. I came and sat next to him and asked to see his cell phone. He kept asking me, "Why do you want to see my cellphone?" I told him, "I want to know who was so important that you needed to be in contact with and we live together and I don't have those numbers."

He looked at me and with a straight face said, "IT'S NOT THAT I CAN'T TELL YOU. I DON'T WANT TO!" It was the first truthful thing that he had ever said to me.

It hit me like a Mack truck, but the reality was there. I didn't cry. I didn't argue. I got up and went upstairs and started neatly packing his stuff. I guess between commercials, he decided to see what I was doing. When he got upstairs he said, "What are you doing?" I replied, "You are leaving here today!"

He began putting all his things back and telling me, "I am not going nowhere! This is my home, too, and it ain't going down like this!"

I kept telling him, "You are going to leave voluntarily or you're going to have help, but you are leaving here today!"

He put all his things back and went back downstairs to watch the game. By me already having experienced an abusive relationship, I got my kids and left. When he finally realized I was gone, he kept calling my cellphone. All I told him is, "It would be best for him to leave my house if he valued his life!"

Even in this situation I was not a cruel person. I was still compassionate. I told him that he could take my Impala and I would give him three months to get it out of my name or return it to me. I knew that his job depended on him having dependable transportation.

When the three months were close, I started trying to contact him. He avoided me for about a week. When I finally did reach him, he told me that he wasn't giving me my car back and I would just have to wait until he improved his credit. I promptly informed him, "When the three months are up and I don't have my car back or you haven't refinanced it, I will definitely report it stolen!" He replied, "Do whatever you are going to do, but I am not giving you your car back and I won't be paying the note or insurance either!"

Just like I told him, I went to the police station on the Westside by his mother's house and tried to report it stolen. The officer at the front desk was a friend of Kurt's and told me that I couldn't report it stolen, because I gave him the keys. He told me I needed to go and see a lawyer because this was a domestic case. His information didn't sit right with me so I went to the police station on the east side by my house and they made my report with no trouble. While leaving the police station, I called Kurt to let him know that the car is now reported stolen. He hung up on me and wouldn't answer the phone anytime I called for about a week. The problem was he knew my schedule so he knew when he could have the car out without me repossessing it.

I ended up getting out of school early and I just prayed about everything. I headed straight over his mother's house with a screwdriver and my steering wheel club. My girl Meka gave me a call while I was in route. She begged me to calm down and to meet her. We met up and I parked my Jeep and rode with her. When we got to his mother's house my car was parked out front on the street. I didn't have an ignition key, but I did have a keyless entry remote. I got out of the car and removed my license plate and put the steering wheel club on and headed up to the police station around the corner from his mother's house. When I walked through the door the same officer was at the front desk. I told him I had reported my car stolen and I have located it and I needed them to go get it for me. He argued with me that I couldn't have reported stolen. His lieutenant came out since we were hollering at each other. He heard my story and told him to look on the stolen list. It was there.

By this time Kurt knew I had been there and was heated. The lieutenant told me to call where the car was and see if Kurt was there and to tell him I was on my way over there to get my keys.

Kurt told me, "Yeah! You come on because I got something for you!"

The lieutenant was listening on speakerphone and grabbed another plainclothes and an undercover police car and followed me to Cheyenne street. When we pulled up, I got out and the officers pulled up on the opposite side of the street. Kurt's nephew, who had just got out of prison, came out the house throwing all kinds of threats. Kurt and his mother were standing at the door. His mother, who before all this jumped off acted like she loved me so much, was cussing me out. The officer walked up to the porch and told Kurt that he needed to give me my keys, because I was the owner of that vehicle. Kurt kept refusing to respond.

The officer said as he pulled his badge out from under his shirt, "You can either give her the keys or you can go to jail tonight and you will be there all weekend at least!"

Needless to say, I got my keys and drove it back to the police station to take it off the stolen list. That was my last real encounter with him and life gets better.

38

The After-Effects

Kurt and I were through, but he hadn't handled anything that we had agreed upon. We had a timeshare in common that I asked him to either remove his name or remove my name, but I refused to pay the note with him still having access to it. I ended up suing him for $5,000.00 in small claims court, but if he has nothing, you can't get it. He already had two child support payments coming out and the government wouldn't take anymore. Kurt also still had his license registered at my address so my car insurance sky-rocketed since he had gotten so many points on his license in a short period of time. I found out that my house and both cars were three months behind.

While I was on disability and he was handling everything, that was just a lie. His nephew that used to live with us was still around the neighborhood and was mad at me, because the three months went for him, too. I started getting threats to burn my Impala up or threatening my life. I called the Impala club members and

102

informed them of what was going on. They put the word out and told me that I am still their sister, THE FIRST LADY, and they wouldn't tolerate it.

I wrote the $5,000 off as a lost on my taxes. I took a loan off my 401k to catch up on my bills, and then I prayed and let MY HEAVENLY FATHER handle the rest. Needless to say, I didn't warm up to the idea of a relationship anytime soon. I vowed that any guy that I dealt with would go through hell dealing with me. I would never let him into my heart so that I can get hurt.

39

My First Birthday Party

My very first birthday party was my 30th birthday. I felt like I had a lot to be thankful for and I wanted to share it with all of my friends. Meka and I had been going to ballroom classes, and Belinda and I had been hitting a few cabarets. So I knew of a cabaret that was three days before my birthday. I got permission to have my birthday party there and bought myself balloons and a cake. I felt the prettiest I have ever felt my whole life. My birthday dress I purchased in Florida. It had spaghetti straps and crossed in the back and it was cut low right above my behind. The dress was a multicolored brown, taupe and cream. My shoes were the thong style heel with sea shells across my foot. I had the same kind of sea shells in my earrings, necklace and anklet. My hair had grown so much with the braids that I was able to wear it in a flip in the back with my hair swooped over my left eye. Every step I took, I got a compliment, and by me loving attention, that was right up my alley. This was the very first time that all of my girlfriends were in the same place together. I remember Meka, Linda, Alisha, Janice, Rochelle, Kim, Taylor, Tim, Robert, Martin, Todd and his brother Arthur and my cousin Derek and his boys. It was the greatest night for me. It was a start of a new beginning for me. I celebrated all the drama that I lived through.

I was thirty and loving it.

40

My Guardian Angel

For some time, I didn't know that I had a guardian angel, but I recall my angel being in my life in the faces of different people. I mean, after looking at all the trials and tribulations I had endured, I know without a shadow of a doubt that I had GOD'S GRACE. My Heavenly Father has always looked out for me even when I didn't know to call on Him.

From the step-child syndrome to the female that every guy I dated cheated on me and had a baby, to the abusive marriage, to the you didn't peep that game and got played, to the recipient of one of GOD'S GREAT GIFTS. I know that I didn't make it through alone. I know that my life has to be a testimony that will help someone else make it through their hard times.

I am not sure yet what my actual purpose is in life, but I will tell you that whatever My Heavenly Father needs from me, I am ready to do. I currently have several different projects open that I have not yet completed, but if GOD wills, they will be successful endeavors. I am at the time in my life that everything I do I ask My Heavenly Father to guide and direct me. I learned that if I build my faith, HE would show how good HE is. Remember that everything happens for a reason, and if you are obedient and freely doing His will, your blessing will be handed to you.

41

My God Sent Gift

One day I received a phone call at my house. It was for my sister Annette. I had just had her moved out of my house. I was so tired of people calling, that I instantly had an attitude. This guy called, "Hello, may I speak to Annette?" I snapped, "Annette don't live here and don't call over here looking for her!"

The guy on the phone paused and said, "Are you okay, Yvonne?" I replied, "You're talking to me like you know me." He said, "This is Tim!" Very sarcastically I replied, "Oh! Wow! I know a bunch of Tim's!" He replied, "You used to date my god-brother."

He sent me for a loop. I couldn't connect the two, then he put his god-brother on the phone. When he said hello, I dropped the phone and jumped back. All the anger, resentment, and hostility melted away.

I got it together and picked up the phone and replied, "Hello!" He inquired was I okay. He told me to take a minute and get myself together. The person on the other

end of the phone was Jericho Victor Caesar. We dated the
summer before my senior year in high school. We sat on
the phone and talked for a couple hours, then we decided
we wanted to meet up. He came over and we sat outside
on the porch and talked for hours more. I couldn't believe
it was him! I always adored him, but when we were
together before I was only seventeen years old and he had
a six-month old daughter he was raising. An altercation
came up between his daughter's mother and me. Instead
of further drama I walked away and avoided his calls. I
mentally couldn't handle the baby-momma drama.

Jericho had a way of making me feel so special. He
still had manners and was polite, with gorgeous brown
eyes and naturally curly hair that he wore in a fade. He
walked with a confidence that totally attracted me to him.
Also, I'd always known him to be good with his hands.
He was never afraid to make some money. Currently he
had two businesses of his own. One was "Jericho of all
Trades," a complete home improvement business. The
other was "Planet Boom," an audio/video automobile
installation company. I knew he worked on cars, because
that's what he was doing when we first met. As of July 22,
2004 we spent every day together, whenever our schedule
allowed.

My friends started to notice a change in me, but no
one had actually met Jericho. I would tell them of the fun
times we have. My friends started telling me that I
sounded like I was in love. I would always dismiss the fact

by saying, "No! He is not my type and what makes you think he is even thinking about me like that?"

I felt like if I kept him out of my heart then I wouldn't get hurt again. My plans were just to enjoy it all while it lasted without getting attached.

One day Jericho and I went up to Blockbuster to see what we hadn't seen. *What A Woman Wants* was a movie on the new-release wall. I picked it up and continued looking for something else. Jericho said, "I know what this woman wants!" I turned and looked at him and smiled as to say Yeah! Right! And asked, "Oh! Really! What do I want?"

We walked from one side of the store to the other and he was still going on with what I want. I finally stopped and turned around and hugged him and said, "Do you really pay that much attention to me?" He was so much on point I couldn't believe it.

That was when the ice around my heart melted. I had prayed for my Heavenly Father to place the man in my life that he wanted me to be with. I vowed that I was not starting another relationship without divine guidance. I also remember my mother always telling me, "You don't find a man that you love. A man finds you and he loves you. Then that is the right man for you."

What are the chances of this man finding me twice and loving me before and now? I know that physically I don't compare to myself at seventeen years old; it's two kids and one abusive marriage later, yet he adores me.

I used to get up and the kids and I would go to church on Sundays, but Jericho would stay home and sleep or watch TV. I wasn't happy with him not sharing that part of my life with me. I started asking him to go, and he gave me several excuses. I let a little time go by then told him, "If you don't love My Heavenly Father how can you love me?" I told him, "My life and the life of my children are more important to me than temporary sexual gratification, and if you don't decide to get off the fence, then we won't even be together for too long."

He explained that he went to a Christian school and there were some things that made him question church. I told him, "Try God and see that He is good. Not every church is the same, but you aren't going for the people. You are going because God is there." I expressed to him how much it meant to me for him to be there with me. I told him I wanted him to have the revelations and testimonies that I have been having. He eventually gave in and attended service with the kids and I on a regular basis.

Well, of course, by now we were very close, and we were living together like a married couple, but dishonoring my Heavenly Father every day. I began getting tired of the constant apologies that I would give to my Heavenly Father. I rationalized, if a child is given rules and they keep breaking the rules, and is knowledgeable of the rules, but always follows it up with, "Please forgive me!" How would I feel as a parent? I would rationalize that you are just defiant and want to do your own thing regardless of what you have been told. At some point, that parent will deal with that disobedient child and I didn't want God to deal with me that way.

I started trying to find out where Jericho's mind was about marriage. He would always tell me, "I am going to marry you, but my God has to let me know that the time is right."

I knew that answer would stay the same as long as I had no follow up response. I eventually asked, "What is the difference with our relationship now and our relationship when we get married? The only difference was that we would legally be committed to one another."

After a few more times asking those questions, I stopped and reasoned either we will be married or we won't. Either he will stay with me or he will leave me, but at some point I have to begin to line up with what My Heavenly Father has told me to do.

One day I sat down and talked to Jericho and told him that we would no longer be having sex, because I wanted to save that for my husband. Nothing else changed in our relationship, but we seemed to be moving farther away from each other. I started praying continuously and removing anything in my life that would hinder my happiness.

It had to be two months later, I remember hugging Jericho, and he looked at me and asked, "Will You marry me?" I replied, "Of course, I already told you I would."

The evening went on as usual. It didn't hit me until a

couple of days later that he might be serious. I sat down and asked him if he was serious when he asked me to marry him? He replied, "Yeah! You're a millennial woman. When you plan the date and get me a ring, we can do this."

My mind was running a million miles per minute. Jericho laid down and took a nap and when he woke up, I had a sticky note that said, "March 11th in Niagara Falls." When he read it he was obviously overwhelmed. He said, "Let's talk about this Friday."

I was so anxious and impatient. I didn't want to wait that long, but I did. When Friday came he pushed our conversation to Monday evening. I started telling my family and close friends that we were getting married in March and it was February. My Godmother, Monica Mills, asked, "Why so fast? Have you all thought about pre-marriage counseling? Why does it have to be in a wedding chapel and not at your church?" I told her that I didn't need a big wedding and didn't need the expenses that would be costly. I figured we just needed to be married instead of living in sin. She agreed with the part about living in sin, but she suggested that I call the church and see if we could be married by the pastor without a ceremony. So I called the church and spoke to Elder Kurtis Tate. He said the same thing about premarital counseling and what was the hurry. (I couldn't tell a minister that I was burning in my flesh and having sex on a regular and enjoying it so much that I am constantly apologizing and repenting, and I just wanted to honor my Heavenly Father in everything.) I listened and walked away very discouraged. Then when I got home and Jericho and I sat down to talk finally. He said the exact same thing about premarital counseling. I looked up to Heaven and said, "Okay, Father, I hear you and I will listen and obey."

I immediately called the church office and made us an appointment for our first session of pre-marriage counseling. After nine sessions, we successfully completed our counseling and received the go-ahead from our Pastor, Marshall L. Walker, and we continued to plan our wedding.

I was a little nervous about planning a complete wedding, seeing we had only until July 23, 2005. Jericho stepped up and told me that he had everything covered. He had the hall, food, decorations and the DJ. I was so surprised. I let him know that whatever he decided would be great, but he still insisted on my opinion. I decided that I wanted to be married by our pastor at our church in the sanctuary. The only other request that I came up with was I wanted the colors to be a pastel rainbow (mint green, sky blue, pale pink, lavender and pale yellow). He handled everything so greatly. He said he had it together and he did! Our wedding was an event to remember. We had a great turn out. It was such an incredible time to see all our friends and family there sharing with us our new beginning.

About the author

Yvonne Campbell was born and raised in Detroit, Michigan the majority of her life. She is an alumnus of Wayne State University where she obtained her Bachelors of Science in Engineering Technology. She worked over 25 years faithfully at AT&T as a large business technician while raising two sons as a single mother. At the peak of her life she met and fell in love with her Lord and Savior, Jesus Christ.

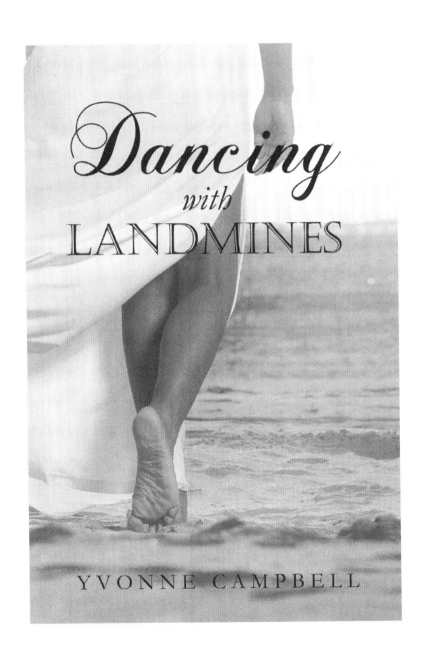

Dancing
with
LANDMINES

YVONNE CAMPBELL

—

Made in the USA
Columbia, SC
16 August 2024

40120277R00079